THE ATTACK ON FORT SUMTER

Charlie Samuels

Gareth Stevens
Publishing

Please visit our website, www.garethstevens.com. For a free color catalog of all our high-quality books, call toll-free 1-800-542-2595 or fax 1-877-542-2596.

Library of Congress Cataloging-in-Publication Data

Samuels, Charlie.
The attack on Fort Sumter / by Charlie Samuels.
  p. cm. — (Turning points in US military history)
Includes index.
ISBN 978-1-4824-0402-9 (pbk.)
ISBN 978-1-4824-0404-3 (6-pack)
ISBN 978-1-4824-0401-2 (library binding)
1. Fort Sumter (Charleston, S.C.) — Siege, 1861 — Juvenile literature. 2. Charleston (S.C.) — History — Civil War, 1861-1865 — Juvenile literature. 3. United States — History — Civil War, 1861-1865 — Causes — Juvenile literature. I. Title.
E471.1 S26 2014
973.731—dc23

Published in 2014 by
Gareth Stevens Publishing
111 East 14th Street, Suite 349
New York, NY 10003

© 2014 Brown Bear Books Ltd

For Brown Bear Books Ltd:
Editorial Director: Lindsey Lowe
Managing Editor: Tim Cooke
Children's Publisher: Anne O'Daly
Design Manager: Keith Davis
Designer: Lynne Lennon
Picture Manager: Sophie Mortimer
Production Director: Alastair Gourlay

Picture Credits:
Front Cover: Library of Congress

All images Library of Congress except:
Boston Public Library: 22; **James Buchanan Resource Center:** 14; **New York State Library:** 29; **Robert Hunt Library:** 43;
Shutterstock: Mesut Dogan 10; **Thinkstock:** Photos.com 24; **U.S. National Archives:** 25, 27, 33.

All Artworks © Brown Bear Books Ltd

Brown Bear Books has made every attempt to contact the copyright holder. If you have any information please contact smortimer@brownbearbooks.co.uk

Manufactured in the United States of America

CPSIA compliance information: Batch #CW14GS. For further information contact Gareth Stevens, New York, New York at 1-800-542-2595.

CONTENTS

INTRODUCTION

Fort Sumter was just one of dozens of forts built around the Atlantic coast of the United States. But when the bitter argument about slavery created a political crisis at the end of 1860, the fate of this small stronghold in Charleston Harbor, South Carolina, gripped the nation. The slave states of the South had left the Union to create the Confederacy. It could not tolerate having a federal military post on its soil. When the first shots were fired at Fort Sumter early on April 12, 1861, the Civil War had begun.

A Welcome War

Many people on both sides were pleased that war had finally come. Both sides believed they could win a rapid victory. Many people perhaps hoped that the fighting would be like the action at Fort Sumter, where there were only a handful of casualties. As the armies took to the battlefield, however, it soon became apparent that the Civil War would be long, hard fought, and very costly in terms of casualties.

War Between Brothers

The fighting would last four years and claim nearly 600,000 lives. The "war between brothers" cast its shadow over the country for decades after the end of the conflict. But the greatest crisis the United States has ever known began in a small corner of a quiet harbor in South Carolina.

Volunteers for the Union Army parade before they head off to fight. There was no shortage of volunteers on either side.

Confederate troops man cannons in Fort Moultrie, in Charleston Harbor, during the shelling of Fort Sumter in April 1861.

The Slavery Debate

By the time Abraham Lincoln was elected president in November 1860, America was deeply divided. States in the South feared the federal government would deny their right to make their own decisions. The main division was about slavery: the power to own other humans as possessions.

Slaves from Africa are sold at an auction in the South. Families were often split up when mothers or fathers were sold to new owners.

Slavery had existed in North America for centuries, but it had been abolished in most northern states by 1804. Many northerners believed slavery was cruel and had no place in a modern, Christian country. The North's manufacturing industries had no need of slaves.

A Slave Economy

In the South, the economy depended on agriculture. Its main crops were cotton, tobacco, and rice. Cotton, in particular, needed many workers to grow. Some 3.5 million black slaves worked on large plantations in the South. Their lives were often hard, and they had few rights.

A BRIEF COMPROMISE

In 1819 Missouri applied to join the Union. There were an equal number of slave and free states, however. Admitting Missouri as a slave state would upset the balance. The US Senate agreed that Missouri would join as a slave state and a new free state (Maine) would be created in northern Massachusetts. This so-called Missouri Compromise of 1820 was based on a line along the southern border of Missouri. Below the line slavery was permitted; above the line, states would be free.

In the early 19th century, the United States expanded dramatically. The Louisiana Purchase (1803) and victory in the Mexican War (1846–1848) added huge new areas into which settlers soon moved. But would the new territories be slave states, like the South, or free states, like the North? The debate threatened to split the country in two.

A Temporary Compromise

In 1820 the so-called Missouri Compromise decreed that for every new slave state, a free state should also be created. But the feeling was growing in the North that slavery was wrong and that the South must ban it. Southerners argued that slavery was a "peculiar institution," and that people outside the

Slaves waiting to be sold were kept in these pens at a slave trader's premises in Alexandria, Virginia.

This print shows an idealized view of plantation life, with white southerners and black slaves living and working together.

South did not understand how it worked. They said that black slaves were inferior people, and that most slave owners treated their slaves well. In reality, southerners feared that the economy would collapse if they had to pay for labor.

End of Compromise

In 1854 the Missouri Compromise was ended by the Kansas–Nebraska Act. The act let settlers in new states decide whether to allow slavery. Kansas became a battleground between the two sides. Then, in 1857, the US Supreme Court ruled against Dred Scott, a slave who wanted to be set free. The decision effectively meant the government could not ban slavery. The anti-slavery abolitionists grew increasingly frustrated.

GROWING VIOLENCE

The shots at Fort Sumter were not the first time the debate over slavery had become violent. While some abolitionists used politics to try to end slavery, others used force. There was so much violence between slavers and abolitionists in Kansas that the state became known as "Bleeding Kansas." In 1856 John Brown, a fanatical abolitionist, killed five proslavery settlers there. His raid on a federal arsenal at Harpers Ferry, Virginia, led to his arrest and execution in 1859.

Abraham Lincoln

Born in a log cabin in Kentucky, Abraham Lincoln was an unlikely man to become the 16th president of the United States. Southerners' distrust of Lincoln helped cause the Civil War, but his leadership saved the country from splitting into two.

This statue of Abraham Lincoln was created for the Lincoln Memorial, which was erected in Washington, DC, in 1922.

Lincoln's mother died when he was just nine, and the family moved to Indiana and then Illinois. Lincoln educated himself and qualified as a lawyer. In 1834, he was elected to the Illinois legislature as a member of the Whig Party. By the 1840s, he was a successful lawyer.

Republican Candidate

Lincoln left the Whigs to join the new Republican Party, which was opposed to the expansion of slavery. Following debates with a Democratic rival in Illinois, Stephen A. Douglas, Lincoln became a national figure. When the Republican Convention met in May 1860, Lincoln won the nomination to stand for the party in the presidential election.

LINCOLN'S DEBATES ABOUT SLAVERY

In 1858 Lincoln ran against Illinois Democrat Stephen A. Douglas to become a senator. Douglas had gotten a bill through Congress to allow settlers in Kansas and Nebraska to decide about slavery for themselves. The two men held seven debates about slavery. While Douglas argued against antislavery legislation in the territories, Lincoln argued powerfully in favor. Although he lost the election, Lincoln's stand helped him win the Republican nomination in 1860.

Lincoln led the country through the Civil War but was assassinated only days after the Confederate surrender.

The Election of 1860

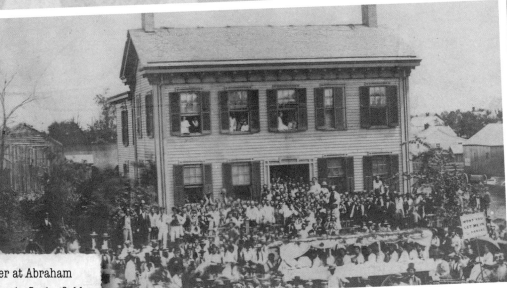

Crowds gather at Abraham Lincoln's home in Springfield, Illinois, in August 1860, after he became the Republican candidate for president.

The 1860 presidential election was dominated by the question of slavery. The Dred Scott case of 1857 had seen the Supreme Court overturn the Missouri Compromise. Both supporters and opponents of slavery were desperate to win the election so that they could enshrine their views in law.

The Democrats fielded two competing candidates: Stephen A. Douglas was by now against slavery, while the Southern Democrat, John C. Breckinridge, wanted to preserve it. Abraham Lincoln stood for the Republican Party.

An Electoral Victory

The election was held on November 6, 1860. Lincoln received 39.8 percent of the popular vote and 180 electoral votes. Stephen Douglas came second, with 29.5 percent. Together, the two antislavery candidates had 69.3 percent of the popular vote. But Lincoln did not receive a single electoral vote from any southern state.

THE REPUBLICAN PARTY

The Democratic Party had dominated politics until activists founded the new Republican Party in 1854. It brought together opponents of slavery from a range of smaller political parties. By 1858, just four years after its first convention, the new party dominated the North. The Republicans came to power with the election of Lincoln in 1860, and would dominate politics until 1932.

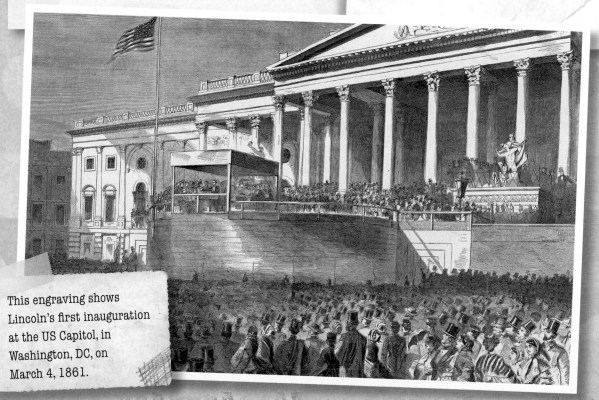

This engraving shows Lincoln's first inauguration at the US Capitol, in Washington, DC, on March 4, 1861.

Secession

Abraham Lincoln's election triggered a reaction in the South, which feared he would abolish slavery. Southerners argued that states had always had the right to secede, or leave the Union. Over six months, 11 states voted to secede. Lincoln's decision to prevent them, by force if necessary, led to the first shots of the war at Fort Sumter.

This northern cartoon shows then-president James Buchanan trying to stop South Carolina and Georgia leaving the Union.

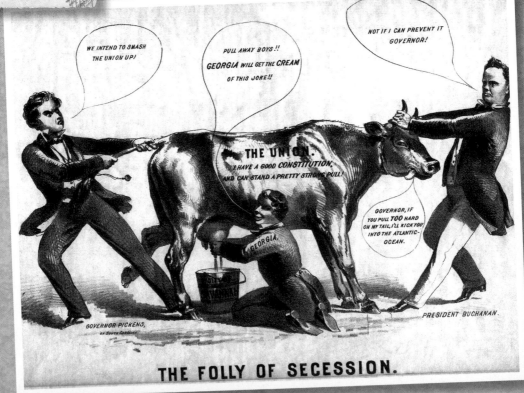

THE FOLLY OF SECESSION.

Democrat supporters of secession for South Carolina meet in Charleston in April 1861.

Secession was not mentioned in the US Constitution. The argument in its favor was based on the idea that the states had rights, which came before the laws of the Union. Early in the 19th century, the leading supporter of this theory was Senator John C. Calhoun of South Carolina. He argued that the state could refuse to follow any federal law it disagreed with.

Rebellion!

In 1832 Calhoun convinced South Carolina not to pay federal tariffs. The state declared it would secede if the government tried to collect the taxes. President Andrew Jackson threatened to send in troops, and the state backed down. Calhoun died in 1850, but by then many southerners believed in the right to secede.

STATES' RIGHTS

The concept of states' rights considers that each state has individual rights within the Constitution, which the national government cannot interfere with. The argument declares that since each state chose to join the Union, it can choose to leave the Union if the federal government does not fulfill its role. Advocates of states' rights believed that the US Constitution left it to each individual state to decide whether or not to allow slavery.

Delegates from the seceding states met in Montgomery, capital of Alabama, to draft a constitution for the new Confederacy.

Although the Republican Party opposed slavery, it promised in the 1860 election campaign not to abolish slavery in existing slave states. It would not, however, allow slavery in new western territories. Many southerners believed that if any new states were free, the balance in Congress would tip against slavery. It would be only a matter of time before the South was forced to give up its slaves and its economy would be ruined.

A Republican President

Southern states believed the election of Abraham Lincoln as the first ever Republican president signaled the beginning of the end of slavery. Once the result of the election was known, states in the South prepared to leave the Union. By February 1, 1861, South Carolina, Mississippi, Florida, Alabama, Georgia, Louisiana, and Texas had all voted to secede. They created the Confederate States of America.

A Second Wave

Southern states that were less dependent on slavery hesitated. But on April 17 the most populous and industrialized southern state, Virginia, voted to secede. Arkansas, North Carolina, and Tennessee followed. Four slave states—Delaware, Kentucky, Maryland and Missouri—never left the Union.

MEETING AT MONTGOMERY

The first seven states to secede met in Montgomery, Alabama, in February 1861 to form a new government. Although eager secessionists were key in creating the Confederacy, the delegates in Montgomery chose more moderate men to lead the new nation. Jefferson Davis of Mississippi became president and Georgia's Alexander H. Stephens was made vice president.

South Carolinians celebrate the decision to leave the Union at a crowded public meeting in Charleston in December 1860.

Davis and the Confederacy

Jefferson Davis was selected as president partly because he was more moderate than many of the most eager secessionists.

On February 18, Jefferson Davis was inaugurated as the first president of the Confederacy. The Confederates wanted to act quickly before Lincoln was sworn in as president of the United States on March 4. Among the urgent issues to resolve was the presence of federal troops in the South—including at Fort Sumter.

This illustration shows President Davis and his cabinet listening to General Robert E. Lee during the course of the war.

The Confederates wanted to send a signal to convince the slave-holding states of the Upper South to join them. They also wanted Britain and France to recognize them as a separate nation. Their new constitution was modeled on that of the Union, but it allowed slavery.

The New President

Jefferson Davis (1808–1889) was a compromise choice as president. He was a Democrat who stood up for southern rights but was known as a moderate. He had an impressive military career and was an experienced politician.

WAIT AND SEE

Not everyone in the South wanted to go to war. Even after the secession of the states in the Deep South, many so-called cooperationists in the Upper South wanted to wait to see what Lincoln would do. They preferred to work with him if possible, rather than leave the Union. There were federal bases throughout the South. If Lincoln decided to resist secession, a military conflict might quickly follow. That was something many people were eager to avoid.

Fortifications

Fort Pickens guarded the harbor at Pensacola, Florida. Although Florida seceded, the fort remained in Union hands during the war.

Before the Civil War, the biggest threat to the United States had been a naval attack by Britain's Royal Navy. To protect the coast, forts were built along the Atlantic seaboard and garrisoned by federal troops. After secession, these forts were suddenly in Confederate territory.

The military tactics of the mid–19th century were based on the creation of forts. These fortifications guarded key harbors around the coast and strategic points on the great rivers of North America. The forts were armed with cannons and permanently manned by troops.

Union Forts

Among the Union strongholds in enemy territory were Fort Sumter, in Charleston Harbor, South Carolina, and nearby Fort Pulaski, at the mouth of the Savannah River in Georgia. The forts were massive stone-and-brick structures, with walls that were 5 feet (1.5 m) thick to withstand attack. Troops lived inside in barracks. Cannons on the fort walls pointed out to sea.

ARTILLERY WEAPONS

Fort walls got thicker as artillery weapons grew more powerful. Coastal forts had to resist the huge guns carried by battleships. These large-caliber, smoothbore cannons could fire long bombardments that would destroy all but the thickest walls. In turn, coastal forts were defended with cannons of their own. The smallest could fire an iron cannonball weighing 32 pounds (14.5 kg) a distance of over 1 mile (1.6 km).

This Union fort is defended by an artillery battery. Fortifications evolved as artillery weapons became more powerful.

South Carolina

It was no coincidence that the first shots of the Civil War were fired in South Carolina. South Carolina was the first state to decide to leave the Union, when its legislators signed the Ordinance of Secession on December 20, 1860. The state's economy was based entirely on slave labor.

This 1861 magazine celebrates the delegates who represented South Carolina at the convention where the Confederacy was created.

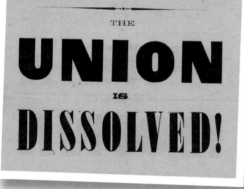

CHARLESTON MERCURY

EXTRA:

Passed unanimously at 1.15 o'clock, P. M., December 20th, 1860.

AN ORDINANCE

To dissolve the Union between the State of South Carolina and other States united with her under the compact entitled " The Constitution of the United States of America."

We, the People of the State of South Carolina, in Convention assembled, do declare and ordain, and it is hereby declared and ordained,

That the Ordinance adopted by us in Convention, on the twenty-third day of May, in the year of our Lord one thousand seven hundred and eighty-eight, whereby the Constitution of the United States of America was ratified, and also, all Acts and parts of Acts of the General Assembly of this State, ratifying amendments of the said Constitution, are hereby repealed; and that the union now subsisting between South Carolina and other States, under the name of " The United States of America," is hereby dissolved.

THE UNION IS DISSOLVED!

The Charleston newspaper announces the passing of the Ordinance of Secession on December 20, 1860.

On Christmas Eve, Governor Francis Wilkinson Pickens declared South Carolina to be separate, independent, and sovereign. The presence of Union troops would not be tolerated.

Seizing Federal Bases

In the two weeks that followed, secessionists seized Fort Moultrie, Castle Pinckney, Fort Jackson, and the arsenal at Charleston without a shot being fired. But federal forces refused to give up Fort Sumter in Charleston Harbor.

JOHN C. CALHOUN

South Carolina's determination to secede reflected the arguments of John C. Calhoun, who had been vice president of the United States from 1825 to 1832. The South Carolinian was a strong supporter of slavery. He promoted a theory called nullification, which argued that each state was sovereign and could therefore declare the US Congress unconstitutional. At the time, Southern states rejected the idea of nullification—but that had changed by the 1860s.

Fort Sumter

Fort Sumter was one of a series of stone fortifications along the Atlantic Coast. It was built in Charleston Harbor, South Carolina, after the War of 1812. As a Union stronghold in a southern state, it became a focus as tensions built between the North and the South.

Fort Sumter stands on an artificial island constructed in Charleston Harbor. Today the fort is a US National Monument.

This photograph shows the interior of Fort Sumter after its surrender. The different levels in the walls were used for cannons.

The fort was a five-sided brick structure built on an artificial island at the entrance to Charleston Harbor. It was designed to hold 650 men and 135 guns, but it was never completed.

Occupying the Fort

Major Robert Anderson commanded federal troops at Fort Moultrie in Charleston Harbor. On December 26, 1860, six days after South Carolina left the Union, he moved his 127 men to Fort Sumter, which he thought would offer more protection against attack. But the fort had only 66 cannons. Worse, its food was running out. Lincoln was reluctant to resupply the fort. He feared the Confederates would see such an action as being provocative.

THE ATLANTIC FORTS

Fort Sumter was just one of a number of fortifications built after independence. They protected the Atlantic seaports from foreign warships, particularly from the British Royal Navy. The forts were the most up-to-date defensive structures in the country. Like Fort Sumter, Fort Pulaski, off Savannah, Georgia, had walls 5 feet (1.5 m) thick. The walls were thick enough to resist cannon fire from enemy ships. The forts' cannons could fire at enemy ships over a mile (1.6 km) away.

Charleston

Although he was reluctant to send supplies, Lincoln also refused to hand over Fort Sumter. That gave Confederate president Jefferson Davis a problem. He could not leave a Union garrison in Confederate territory. But if he did not act, South Carolina's secessionists might try to capture the fort.

Charleston was one of the major ports in the South, so the Confederates were eager to keep it open to shipping for trade.

Pierre G. T. Beauregard fought in every theater of the Civil War and became one of only eight full generals in the Confederacy.

RESPECTFUL ENEMIES

When Brigadier General Pierre G. T. Beauregard arrived in Charleston, he set about improving the harbor defenses. Beauregard knew the commander of Fort Sumter, Major Robert Anderson, who had taught him at the military academy at West Point. The two men had great respect for each other. Beauregard sent fine cigars and other gifts to the fort, but Anderson ordered them to be sent back. The eventual surrender of the fort made Beauregard a hero throughout the Confederacy.

On December 27, 1860, Governor Francis Pickens ordered South Carolina militia to occupy the other forts in Charleston Harbor, including the poorly defended Fort Moultrie and Castle Pinckney, which stood at the mouth of the Cooper River. The long-abandoned Fort Johnson on James Island was also reoccupied.

Artillery Target

Davis now ordered General Pierre G. T. Beauregard to take charge of all the forts. Confederate troops set up artillery batteries around the harbor, in the newly seized forts, and on an ironclad ship. Beauregard gave Major Robert Anderson at Fort Sumter a final deadline to surrender by 4:30 A.M. on April 12, 1861.

Inside the Fort

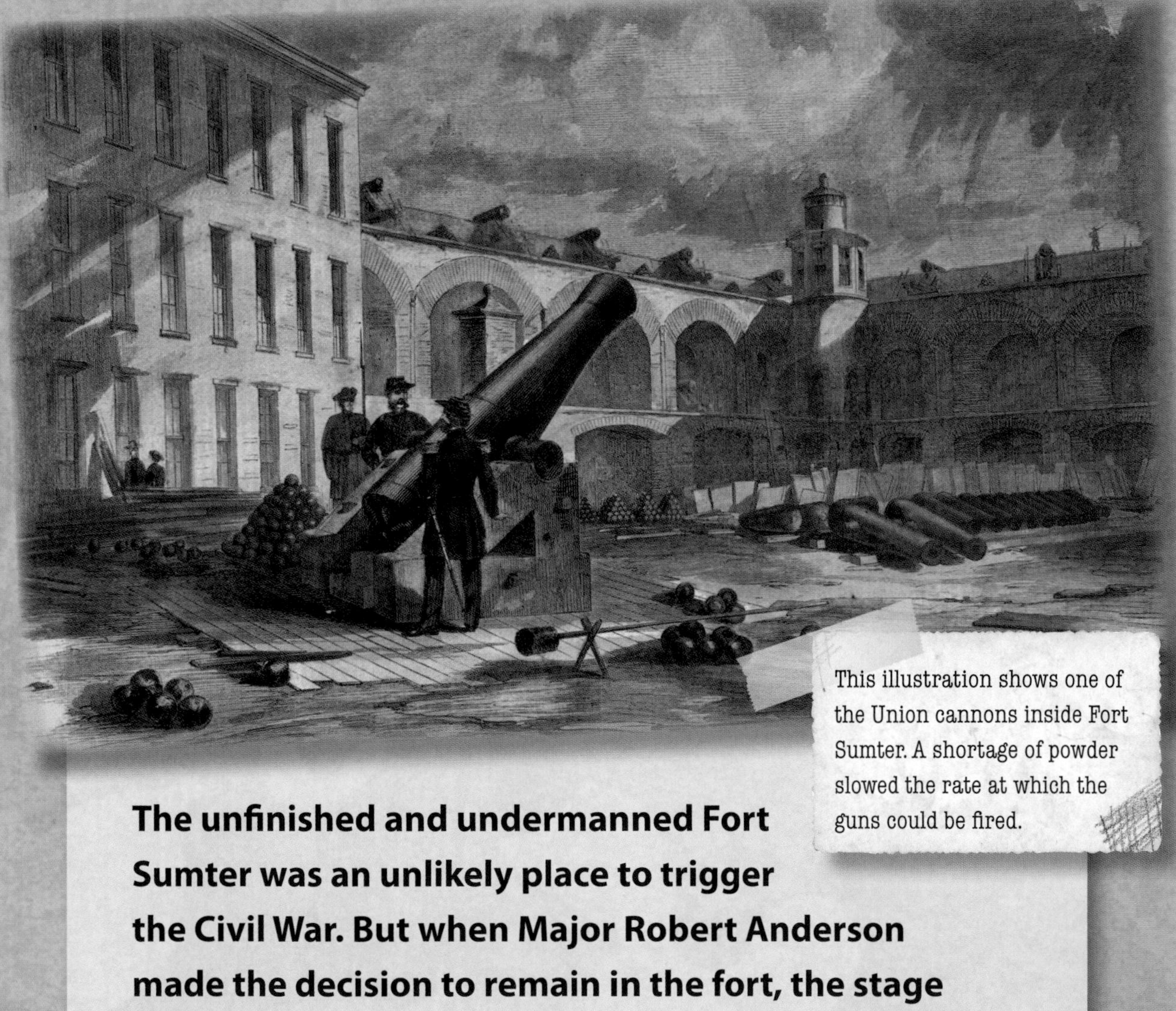

This illustration shows one of the Union cannons inside Fort Sumter. A shortage of powder slowed the rate at which the guns could be fired.

The unfinished and undermanned Fort Sumter was an unlikely place to trigger the Civil War. But when Major Robert Anderson made the decision to remain in the fort, the stage was set for a showdown. Anderson's men were the last Union troops in Confederate territory.

On December 27, 1860, Francis Pickens, the governor of South Carolina, ordered Anderson to leave Fort Sumter and return to Fort Moultrie. Anderson refused. The US government sent the ship *Star of the West* with supplies. On January 9, 1861, South Carolina artillery fired on the ship as it entered Charleston Harbor. The vessel withdrew.

Disobeying Orders

Anderson and his 127 men were then barricaded in the fort with no prospect of being resupplied. But they refused to surrender.

MAJOR ROBERT ANDERSON

Robert Anderson was a former slave owner from Kentucky who stayed loyal to the Union. When South Carolina seceded, he commanded US troops in Charleston. His bravery in refusing to surrender Fort Sumter made him a national hero in the North. He was promoted to brigadier general and briefly commanded Union troops in Kentucky before being reassigned. He retired in 1863.

This contemporary engraving shows Major Robert Anderson and the officers who served with him at Fort Sumter.

First Shots of the War

As his supplies ran low and tension grew, Anderson desperately played for time. He tried to delay negotiations to give Union supply ships time to arrive. But the Confederates were running out of patience and finally opened fire. Anderson's firepower could not compete with that of his enemy.

Smoke rises as Confederate shells fall on Fort Sumter. The 36-hour artillery bombardment eventually left the fort in ruins.

Abner Doubleday was Anderson's second-in-command in the fort. He fired the first Union shot.

MARY CHESNUT, AN EYEWITNESS

"At half-past four the heavy booming of a cannon.... The shells were bursting.... I knew my husband was rowing about in a boat somewhere in that dark bay, and that the shells were roofing it over, bursting toward the fort. If Anderson was obstinate, Colonel Chesnut was to order the fort on one side to open fire. Certainly fire had begun. The regular roar of the cannon, there it was. And who could tell what each volley accomplished of death and destruction?"

Forced to make a decision, President Lincoln sent a fleet of Union ships to resupply Fort Sumter. They arrived at Charleston Harbor on April 12, 1861. It was too late. The previous day Beauregard had sent three aides to demand the surrender of the fort. Anderson had refused.

A Last Chance

At 3:20 A.M. on April 12, Colonel James Chesnut and Captain Stephen Lee rowed to Fort Sumter to give Anderson a final chance to surrender. Again, he refused. Now Chesnut headed to Fort Johnson.

A Confederate battery fires on Fort Sumter on April 13, 1861. Low on ammunition, the fort surrendered later that afternoon.

Chesnut ordered the Confederate artillery to open fire. The first shell was fired at 4:30 A.M. but the bombardment would continue for 36 hours. Private Edmund Ruffin, a wealthy plantation owner, claimed to have fired the first shot. In fact, it may have come from a battery on James Island.

The Union Response

The Union response did not start until around 7:00 A.M. because the fort was so short of ammunition. The first shot was fired by Captain Abner Doubleday. With so little ammunition, Union soldiers could only fire occasionally. Firing went on throughout the day, but that night the fort's guns fell silent while the Confederates kept firing.

Edmund Ruffin may have fired the first shot of the Civil War—but today his claim to have done so is sometimes disputed.

EDMUND RUFFIN

Edmund Ruffin was one of the wealthiest men in Virginia, owning a number of plantations and a hundred slaves. He was a long-standing supporter of the South's separation from the North. When Abraham Lincoln was elected to the presidency, Ruffin refused even to stay in Virginia. Instead he moved to South Carolina. Ruffin claimed that Colonel James Chesnut gave him the honor of firing the first shot against his hated northerners. Today some people doubt this claim.

Next day Anderson surrendered. He was low on gunpowder and had no provisions left. Anderson's Union men marched out of the badly-burned fort with the colors flying and the drums beating.

Fatal Salute

Anderson's mens fired a 50-gun salute to the Union flag. One of the cannons misfired, causing the only two Union deaths of the battle. One Confederate had also been killed by a misfiring cannon.

Anaconda Plan

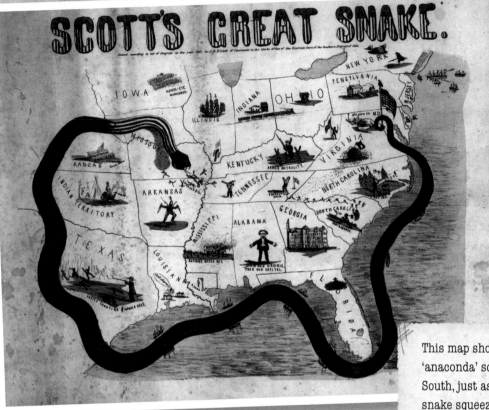

This map shows Scott's 'anaconda' squeezing the South, just as the anaconda snake squeezes its victims to death.

One reason Fort Sumter was so important was the North's strategy for fighting the Civil War. It planned to cut the Confederacy off from all overseas trade so that it would be forced to surrender or starve. For that, the North had to control the South's coastline.

President Lincoln ordered a naval blockade of Confederate ports. His commander in chief, Winfield Scott, planned to shut down all Atlantic trade. He would then gain control of the Mississippi to cut off the western Confederacy.

One Step Ahead

Scott's blockade plan was based on two key factors. First, the US Army was not very large. Second, he did not want to completely destroy the South. The plan was unpopular in the North. People wanted a quick victory, not a slow blockade.

New Yorkers stage a great patriotic rally in Union Square on April 20, 1861, a week after the shelling of Fort Sumter.

WINFIELD SCOTT

US commander in chief Winfield Scott was almost 75 years old at the start of the war. During the secession crisis, he advised Abraham Lincoln to surrender Fort Sumter but the president rejected the idea. Scott was too old and sick to command for long. After the defeat at Bull Run in July 1861, he retired. But he did live long enough to see Union victory.

Raising the Troops

Infantry from the 134th Illinois Regiment drill after joining up. Drill taught troops to act as a single unit in battle.

When Fort Sumter fell to the Confederates, the Union army had just 16,000 regular troops. The Confederate army was barely a month old. With the sudden arrival of war, both sides had to raise and train troops as quickly as possible.

This recruiting poster from New Jersey offers cash bounties, or payments, for volunteers who enlist for the Union army.

PUBLIC OPINION

After the fall of Fort Sumter, southerners were confident they would enjoy a quick victory over the North. In the same way, the loss of the fort made northerners more determined to defeat the South. Public support for the war in the North remained strong apart from two serious dips when the military campaign was going badly in the summer and fall of 1862. In the South, white southerners remained behind the Confederate cause for the length of the war.

Volunteer Forces

Both sides initially relied on volunteers but later used the draft to recruit soldiers. In the North, recruitment began the day after Fort Sumter fell, on April 15, 1861. When Lincoln called for 75,000 men, 91,000 men volunteered. Later in the war, each state raised a specific quota of troops via a draft.

The Confederate army was made up of militiamen and volunteers, who each signed up for 12 months. The troops barely had enough equipment, clothing, or food. Their morale was high, however.

Battle of Bull Run

Union infantry fire a volley at Bull Run. The men in red pants are Zouaves, who wore uniforms based on French units in North Africa.

The gunfire at Fort Sumter marked the start of the Civil War. The public on both sides were eager to fight. But the first major battle of the war, fought in northern Virginia, showed that they were mistaken to think that the war would be a short one.

By July 1861, the Union army numbered 35,000, while the Confederates had about 20,000 men. In July the Union army advanced to Manassas, a key Confederate railroad depot in northern Virginia. The Confederates retreated behind Bull Run Creek.

A Heavy Cost

On July 21, the two sides finally met in a battle that was won by the arrival by train of 10,000 Confederate reinforcements. The Union troops retreated to Washington, DC. Combined casualties were about 5,000. It was clear that the coming conflict would be hard fought and would cost many lives.

STONEWALL JACKSON

Confederate hero Thomas "Stonewall" Jackson got his nickname at Bull Run. His Virginia Brigade held their position during a Union attack— standing "like a stone wall." Jackson was one of the South's greatest generals. He was a brilliant tactician known for daring strikes on Union troops. He died when he was mistakenly shot by his own men at the Battle of Chancellorsville in 1863.

Stonewall Jackson (with black hat and sword) and his officers watch as the fighting unfolds along Bull Run Creek.

The Course of the War

The Civil War was fought in two main theaters. In the east, the South tried to advance on Washington, DC, and the North targeted Richmond, Virginia. In the west, fighting focused on the Mississippi Valley, which held the Confederacy together.

A narrow victory at the Battle of Shiloh in April 1862 was the first step in the Union conquest of the Mississippi River.

Union soldiers attack during the siege of Vicksburg in summer 1863. The fall of the city split the Confederacy in two.

After the Battle of Bull Run, the war in the east entered a relatively quiet period. The Union concentrated on establishing a naval blockade of the South. It also tried to take control of the Mississippi River in order to cut the Confederacy in two. But after a narrow victory at the Battle of Shiloh in April 1862, Union forces were held up by the strong Confederate position at Vicksburg.

Defeat at Antietam

In summer 1862, Union forces attempted to advance on the Confederate capital, Richmond, Virginia. They were driven back by the new Confederate commander, Robert E. Lee. In fall, Lee invaded the North but was defeated at Antietam in Maryland.

ROBERT E. LEE

The outstanding general of the Civil War was the Confederate Robert E. Lee, who took command of the Army of Northern Virginia in summer 1862. Lee came from one of Virginia's leading slave-owning families and was a graduate of West Point. He was widely admired for his aggressive tactics. After his army was beaten at Gettysburg, however, Lee knew it was over for the Confederacy. After the war, he spent his remaining years working for reconciliation between the North and South.

Confederate infantry march across open ground during "Pickett's Charge," a turning point of the Battle of Gettysburg.

After the Union victory at Antietam, President Lincoln announced a preliminary Emancipation Proclamation. This declared that all slaves in states fighting the Union would be freed on January 1, 1863. This made ending slavery a goal of the war. It also made it impossible that the Confederacy would gain international recognition. No European country wanted to be seen to be supporting slavery.

Reverse and Defeat

In July 1863 Union forces captured Vicksburg and won control of the Mississippi. Lee launched another Confederate invasion of the North, but he was defeated in a three-day battle at Gettysburg, Virginia. The battle became known as the "high-water mark of the Confederacy." After Gettysburg, the South was always on the defensive. Union general

William T. Sherman captured Atlanta in the west then marched east through Georgia and the Carolinas, bringing devastation to wide areas.

Surrender of the South

Lee could not stop a northern advance on Richmond. He surrendered to Ulysses S. Grant at Appomattox on April 9, 1865. The war that began at Fort Sumter had lasted nearly four years. More than 600,000 Americans had died and 400,000 had been wounded—but the Union had survived.

FORT SUMTER

The surrender was not Fort Sumter's last part in the war. In April 1863, Union ships began bombarding the fort during efforts to recapture Charleston Harbor. The Confederates strengthened the fort, which also withstood an attempted landing. The bombardment continued, and the fort was badly damaged. In February 1865, Sherman's march through South Carolina forced the Confederates to evacuate Charleston. Fort Sumter was abandoned, and its ruins were reclaimed by the Union.

General Robert E. Lee (right) surrenders to General Ulysses S. Grant at Appomattox Court House on April 9, 1865.

TIMELINE

1820 The Missouri Compromise sets out to balance the number of slave and free states in the Union.

1854 The Kansas–Nebraska Act ends the Missouri Compromise by allowing settlers to choose whether new states allow slavery.

1856 May: The abolitionist John Brown kills five proslavery settlers on raids in Kansas.

1857 In the Dred Scott case, the US Supreme Court upholds the legality of slavery.

1858 During an Illinois senatorial campaign, Abraham Lincoln makes a national impact when debating against slavery with his opponent, Stephen A. Douglas.

1859 October: John Brown leads a raid on a federal arsenal at Harper's Ferry, Virginia, in the hopes of starting a slave revolt. The raid fails and Brown is hanged.

1860 November: Abraham Lincoln is elected president.
December 20: South Carolina votes to secede from the Union.

1861 January 2: Confederate troops occupy forts in Charleston Harbor.
January: Mississippi, Florida, Alabama, Georgia, and Louisiana leave the Union.
February 4: The Confederate Congress chooses Jefferson Davis as president.
March 4: Abraham Lincoln is inaugurated as the 16th president.
April 12: Confederates attack Fort Sumter in Charleston Harbor.

April 13: Fort Sumter surrenders.
April 15: Abraham Lincoln calls for volunteers to raise a 75,000-strong army.
April 19: Lincoln orders a naval blockade of the southern states.
July 21: The First Battle of Bull Run is a narrow victory for the Confederates.

1862   March 17: Union troops begin the Peninsular Campaign in Virginia.
April 7: The Battle of Shiloh ends with neither side achieving gains.
August 14: Union troops abandon the Peninsular Campaign.
September 17: The inconclusive Battle of Antietam is fought in Maryland.
September 22: Lincoln issues the Emancipation Proclamation, to take effect on January 1, 1863.

1863   January: Two Confederate ironclads break the Union blockade of Charleston.
May 18: Union troops begin the siege of Vicksburg.
June 16: Robert E. Lee's army invades the North.
July 3: Lee's advance is halted at Gettysburg in the war's largest battle.
July 4: Vicksburg surrenders, splitting the Confederacy in two.
September: Union assaults in Charleston Harbor capture Fort Wagner but not Fort Sumter.

1864   August 31: General William T. Sherman cuts supply lines at Atlanta, Georgia, which falls the next day. Sherman sets out to march through the South.
December 21: Sherman reaches Savannah, Georgia, ending the "March to the Sea."

1865   January 19: Sherman's troops enter South Carolina.
April 3: Confederates retreat from their capital, Richmond.
April 9: Robert E. Lee surrenders to General Grant at Appomattox Court House in Virginia.
April 14: Abraham Lincoln is shot while at the theater and dies the next day.

GLOSSARY

artillery Heavy weapons such as cannons, which can fire heavy shells long distances.

battery A group of artillery weapons operating together in the same position.

blockade Measures aimed at preventing trade by using ships to intercept vessels heading to port.

colors The flag of a military unit.

compromise An agreement in which both sides make concessions in order to settle their differences.

delegation A group of representatives at a meeting.

federal Relating to the government of the United States of America.

fort A fortified position defended by soldiers.

garrison To use a group of soldiers, or garrison, to occupy a military post.

ironclad A warship covered in iron plates for protection.

morale The fighting spirit of an individual or group, and how much they believe in victory.

quota A required quantity.

secession Breaking away from a union. States that seceded from the Union formed the Confederacy.

siege A military action in which forces surround an enemy position or town in order to force it to surrender.

strategy A plan that relates to an overall conflict, rather than to a short-term victory in a battle.

tactics How commanders arrange and move their forces during a battle.

volley The simultaneous firing of many weapons, especially rifles.

Zouave A member of a colorfully dressed military unit based on Algerian units in the French army.

FURTHER INFORMATION

Books

Burgan, Michael. *Fort Sumter* (We the People). Compass Point Books, 2006.

Fay, Gail. *Battles of the Civil War* (Heinemann Infosearch). Heinemann Raintree, 2010.

Golay, Michael. *Civil War* (America at War). Chelsea House Publications, 2010.

Kent, Zachary. *The Civil War: From Fort Sumter to Appomattox* (The United States at War). Enslow Publishers, 2011.

Puttnam, Jeff. *A Nation Divided: Causes of the Civil War* (Understanding the Civil War). Crabtree Publishing Co., 2011.

Wagner, Heather Lehr. *The Outbreak of the Civil War: A Nation Tears Apart* (Milestones in American History). Chelsea House Publishers, 2008.

Websites

www.civilwar.si.edu
Civil War collections from the Smithsonian Institution, with articles, photographs, and other primary sources.

www.pbs.org/civilwar
PBS site supporting the Ken Burns documentary *The Civil War.*

www.civilwar.com
Privately run, moderated site with comprehensive resources about the Civil War.

www.historyplace.com/civilwar
Civil War timeline on The History Place website.

Publisher's note to educators and parents: Our editors have carefully reviewed these websites to ensure that they are suitable for students. Many websites change frequently, however, and we cannot guarantee that a site's future contents will continue to meet our high standards of quality and educational value. Be advised that students should be closely supervised whenever they access the Internet.

INDEX